Cozy
Interiors

AUTHOR
Jessica Lawson

EDITORIAL DIRECTOR
Nacho Asensio

TEXTS
Patricia Bueno

DESIGN AND LAYOUT
Carlos Gamboa Permanyer

COVER DESIGN
Núria Sordé Orpinell

ENGLISH TRANSLATION
Peter Miller

PRODUCTION
Juanjo Rodríguez Novel

Published by: Atrium Group de ediciones y publicaciones, S.L.
c/ Ganduxer, 112
08022 Barcelona

Telf : +34 932 540 099
Fax : +34 932 118 139
e-mail : atrium@atriumgroup.org
www.atriumbooks.com

ISBN: 84-95692-35-X
D.L.: B-07868-03

Printed in Spain
ANMAN Gràfiques del Vallès, S.L.

Cozy
Interiors

contents

introduction

The same thing happens with houses as with people: there are some with whom, without really knowing why or how, we spontaneously establish affectionate ties. They are houses, environments, people, which manage to bring out the best in us.

Cozy Interiors puts forward multiple ideas which reveal that mystery, that why and how. In fact, creating an environment which transmits positive energy to us, which helps us to feel that we have found our place in the world, is not as difficult as it seems. Basically, two ingredients are needed: on the one hand, affection, choosing each piece, each fabric, every light and every shade, aware that from now on they will form part of our lives, and, on the other hand, sufficient sensitivity to be able to perceive the "soul" of the things and shapes that surround us.

Affection and sensitivity are, therefore, the base on which all the images that illustrate this book have been chosen. In each case, the decoration is made to measure for the people who live in it, establishing a symbiotic dialogue, in virtue of which the one would not be possible without the other. That is to say, it is a living decoration, where each object occupies its precise place in relation to the others and in relation to the specific circumstances that define, at that moment, the inhabitants of the house.

In the words of the poet Hölderlin, "man inhabits poetically". This means that he establishes poetic, symbolic and emotional relationships with the objects that surround him, beyond their functionality and the simple reality of shapes and colors. In an environment of poetic nuances, each thing has its symbology, whether abstract or precise, turning into metaphors with highly suggestive power.

Each of the nooks in our house is susceptible to becoming our favorite, where we do not notice the passing of time, where we would like to stay forever, hiding away from everybody else. That is what this book is about, converting the space where we live into an intimate paradise, our own private, personal and unique shelter. The challenge is to transform the "noise" in which we are constantly wrapped up outside, into a relaxing melody with which we can feel identified, which transmits notes of familiarity and peace to us, where we can take refuge and feel protected.

Beginning with the lounge, a place for gatherings, hospitality and intimate conversations, "Cozy Interiors" continues its evocative journey through the bedroom, the kitchen, the bathroom and outside the house. In each of the chapters, corresponding to each of the rooms, many examples are included of rooms with magic, a certain spark, with the power of suggestion and the power to send us to a place close to the heart. Each picture tells a particular story, starting out from the coexistence of the different elements. From each of them, we can draw our own conclusions, as if it was the moral of a fairy tale. Perhaps, in one of them, we could fall in love with a combination of colors or a pigment. In another, we are surprised by the simple beauty of a stone floor, or the subtlety of some linen curtains diffusing the light at sundown. In the next one, we are entrapped by the imaginative recovery of an old piece of furniture —used on numerous occasions to fulfill a very different function from that for which it was created—, or the clever use of an architectural resource, capable of transforming the general appearance of the room.

What they all have in common, apart from their visual richness, is what the title of the book indicates: they are cozy, they transmit serenity and well being. We all feel the need to have our own place with these characteristics, which allows us to escape from the standardization of the world around us, from the ordinary, from mass manufacture, from the impersonal. It is a question of being patient, of losing ourselves in grandma's attic, of checking out (remember, with affection and sensitivity) markets and antique stores, of investing more time than money in the decoration of our house, which will have a direct effect on the particular story that each person wants to tell.

PATRICIA BUENO

peaceful time

 Who cares about fashions? That this season the color chocolate and white lacquered furniture are in? That fabrics come with big flowery prints or embroidered butterflies? The really important thing is not what the trends of the moment dictate, but finding our own style, capable of going beyond any moment, any time.

To be precise, timeless is the adjective that best defines the following lounges and dining rooms, suspending in a limbo space that knows nothing of clocks or calendars. This is the magic of rooms that mix elements from the rustic style with others inspired by the classical forms, seasoned with details of an unclassifiable style, which can only be identified with the personality of each person.

There are details and gestures capable of introducing, by themselves, warmth in the room, radically changing the appearance of our lounge or dining room without needing large investments: Painting the walls with natural pigments, paving the floor with earthenware tiles or stone, or covering it with a rug with oriental accents, renewing the sofa's upholstery or, simply, putting a lively colored throw over it, with a certain casual air; situating plants and flowers strategically around the room; changing the lighting, so that it imitates the reflections of natural light; creating a nice corner for reading, where the pleasant figure of an armchair stands out; recovering a forgotten piece of furniture, giving it another chance...; are just a few examples of actions that can modify our way of looking at life, gazing from a comfortable sofa at the way time passes without fraying our edges.

The aim is to seek a balance, to find compositions that are in harmony with the surroundings and nature, that invite us to forget rushing about and that the world turns and turns without ever stopping. Once this challenge has been met, memory will undertake the completion of a perfect atmosphere, by conjuring up intimate moments lived within those walls, whether past, present or future.

WHITE AND STONE.
Often, elegance resides in simplicity. A whitewashed wall, a wicker armchair with some books at its feet,
a linen curtain that plays with the air, a center table found in a flea market, a wall covered with stone, some armchairs
with white linen covers around a basic fireplace (where one could say we have found a new decorative style: rustic minimalism).
Places where it is easy to imagine turning the pages of a novel or having lively conversations with friends, which always end up
trying to find the best course of action to put the world to rights.

For ever and ever.
Some elements of the classical and rustic style have the same gift as the chameleon: they are capable of keeping themselves safe
from evolution's assault, blending in with the environment and integrating perfectly in 21st Century atmospheres.
They can be inherited pieces of furniture or acquired in some local antique shop, but in any case they give off a certain aura of familiarity
and respect for the past, which converts them into a link between our ancestors and the present moment. What's more, who cannot find
in their lounge a corner to house an armchair with classic lines, with the aristocratic poise of bygone ages?

CHANGE OF IMAGE.
An excellent resource for renovating the image of our lounge, without having to make big changes or invest heavily, is to upholster our old sofa —and for sofa, read chaise-longue, pouffe, chair, stool or armchair—, with a intensely colored, youthful and up-to-date fabric. This simple operation is capable of turning the appearance of this room right around, changing its plastic arts force. In these examples, fuchsia has been the chosen color, but the same effect can be achieved with reds, greens, oranges, mauves..., and any tone that suits us best, just as long as it transmits energy.

NATURAL PIGMENTS.

Another way of drastically changing the appearance of lounges and dining rooms, giving them a much warmer appearance, is by painting the walls with colors taken from nature, applied using a traditional method, such as with a sponge. The most successful pigments, because they always give good results, are ochres and terracottas. They present a wide range of tonalities, from the most intense ones to those that are barely perceptible, and it is difficult to become tired of them. Another of their qualities is that they combine well with the majority of colors, bringing out the shapes of furniture and complements thanks to the contrast with the colored background.

DISTANT ECHOES.

*Ethnic inspirations leave a veneer of old flavor over these rooms, of stories told with different accents, of cultures
living together, with the enrichment that this involves. Sometimes, a small detail is enough to make our imagination fly towards
other countries and peoples: a hand woven rug with drawings loaded with symbology; an oriental-style low table, representing
a whole philosophy of life, an African mask, indicative of a distant ritual... they are objects with an enormous capacity
for evocation, which makes us feel at home even though they come from far away.*

ARCHES AND OPEN SPACES.
The lounge and dining room are two rooms with set functions, which can be interpreted in different ways: as a single space where the two concepts are integrated, as two separate rooms or introducing some element which separates them visually, but not physically, managing to preserve the spaciousness that is inherent in the first option. In the latter case, an architectural retouching as simple as the creation of an arch achieves a result which is very effective aesthetically. Two more ideas to note down: 1. Use cotton covers on the chairs, an economical way to renovate the appearance of the dining room. 2. To invest in contemporary art.

PALMA CIUDAD DE PATIOS
LA CASA Y EL TIEMPO

REINTERPRET A CLASSIC.
When we think of an ancient roman, we imagine him lying on a couch or chaise-longue, sampling exquisite delicacies. It is curious to see that this piece of furniture for sitting on still maintains part of its connotations of nobility. And the thing is, invariably, whether it is reminiscent of classicism or has an avant-garde design, the chaise-longue becomes the queen of the lounge. A springy filling and an upholstery pleasant to the touch and the eye, like the equally noble velvet, make it more in accordance with current necessities: looking at the world from a chaise-longue one can converse, read, watch television, have afternoon tea, take a nap or sleep, should an extra bed be necessary.

MIXTURE OF CONCEPTS.
When done with just the right doses, the mixture of elements creates perfectly coherent compositions. A house built according to the classical or rustic canons can be decorated without following the same criteria. It could even generate greater visual dynamism to include a modern design sofa, or an emblematic piece of contemporary design, complemented with objects of romantic reminiscence or influenced by the style of other countries. It is a question of combining furniture and complements with wisdom and balance, without committing the sin of excess and going to extremes.

MAKE THE MOST OF SPACE.
If we make good use of the available meters, it is possible to integrate lounge, dining room and kitchen in a reduced space, managing to make the whole thing cozy without it being overloaded. In this case, the room's corner has been taken advantage of to install a small kitchen.

CONTRASTS, CONTRASTS.
Another good example of a corner whose charm comes from eclecticism. A classically designed sofa presides over the room, accompanied by an oriental kilim, some cushions which serve as a small table and a series of paintings which contribute a contemporary accent. Perfect.

THE LANGUAGE OF PLANTS, FLOWERS AND FABRICS.

A simple little bunch of flowers, some fresh lilies or some intensely green plants are capable of transmitting deep feelings and introducing a small part of the force of nature inside the house. It is a beautiful custom to periodically renew the flowers in the lounge, bringers of light and joy. Fabrics also have the same capacity to grant our lounge different meanings, whether by their color or their design, as well as by the material from which they have been woven: silk, linen, cotton, wool, leather, brocade, velvet, chenille, damask...
are materials and textures that bring diverse connotations.

canopies, beams and other caprices

 Perhaps the bedroom is the most favorable space to set free our most romantic and dreamy side. It is the place of regeneration and sincerity, where we feel in direct contact with ourselves, without intermediaries or affectations. So why not allow ourselves the caprices, subtleties or emotional flights of fancy that we do not allow ourselves in the rest of our environment?

From these pages, we commit ourselves to the creation of an atmosphere like that of a poem written at sundown, impregnated with romantic details that make this room a place where we can allow our feelings and passions free rein. In these rooms, nature takes on a special importance, becoming the element capable of transporting us to another world, far from all our obligations, and exchanging the color gray of the city for the aromas of lavender from Provence in France.

Children also have their space in these pages, with bedrooms full of color and fantasy, that stimulate their senses and accompany their innate capacity to daydream, playing at being the protagonists of their favorite movie.

There are many resources which can be used to transform the bedroom into a personal version of a fairy tale. Linen curtains with delicate embroidery that flirt with the morning breeze, traditional *boutí* bedspreads with floral prints, capturing springtime in their folds; beds with canopies, or with cool mosquito nets, which wrap and protect our dreams with diaphanous fabrics; headboards and legs made of carved or polychrome wood, which value traditional workmanship, chests of drawers and bedside tables rescued from an antique shop, adding a touch of history; bunches of wild flowers, pastel tones on a white background; ceilings with wooden beams; and souvenirs, books, found objects, light, imagination, wishes and things to tell.

Looking at these photos, the world is contemplated from a different perspective: romanticism is in the air.

FAIRY TALES.

Although we lose the capacity to dream about fairy tale princes and princesses as we get older, we always have the compensation of waking up each morning in a bucolic atmosphere, where we can even put a dressmaker's dummy as a decorative element, with a dress fit for Cinderella resting upon it. With some well-chosen complements, it will not be necessary to rely on the spells of a fairy godmother to transform this room into a magical place. An embroidered bedspread, some wall lights or little lamps which project a cozy light, some graceful bedside tables...

DREAMING IN COLOR.
Children's bedrooms are a world apart. They are the perfect terrain to give free reign to fantasy. They are the kingdom of color and impossible compositions. As the children grow, walls start to be decorated with their works of art, and soft toys and dolls become permanent guests. Their little possessions also grow, so that it is necessary to increase storage surface. A made-to-measure shelf unit, where numerous wicker baskets fit, is an excellent solution to the problem of maintaining everything in order, making the most of the available meters without renouncing aesthetics.

CREATIVE SOUL.

Walls and floors become play surfaces, where the little ones can give expression to their creativity with freedom. A blackboard and a large roll of paper hanging from the wall turn the walls into large canvases, while the floor has become a game board. An old clothes closet has completely changed its image and function, to become integrated in this recreational room, shaking off its traditional seriousness when covered in a luminous blue color. Everything is allowed to boost imagination and stimulate the children's creativity and desire to play.

A RAY OF SUNSHINE.

Natural light is a source of life, which is why it is important that it should be the first thing to wish us good morning when we wake up, helping us with its energy to get out of bed with optimism. It is also worth taking into account the variations that sunlight goes through during the day, and the different way it will behave with the fabrics and materials we have chosen. Some light linen curtains are ideal for diffusing direct sunlight, without preventing it entering the bedroom. On the other hand, the white colored or floral print bedclothes intensify the luminosity of the room.

CHESTS OF DRAWERS AND BRAZIER TABLES.

Recuperating classic furniture that used to form part of the bedroom, accompanying them with a rustic atmosphere or with up-to-date complements, allows us to preserve the charm of traditional bedrooms, at the same time giving them a more youthful appearance. One of the items of furniture which most often crop up in our memory are chests of drawers, which with their imposing presence usually share the leading role with the bed. Brazier tables, with long, thick tablecloths that hide their structure, also form part of the old universe of the bedroom, generally creating a harmonious group with the headboard of the bed and the cushions and curtains.

RED SQUARES.
In this picture, the fabric with red checks lends itself to form part of a classical composition, on which it impresses a jovial character.
The lampshade, the armchair and the bedspread have been made from the same fabric, unifying the diverse elements.

BLUE SQUARES.
Meanwhile, the blue and white checks are perfectly integrated in this rustic ambience, where the structure of the room itself stands out,
with unpolished whitewashed walls and attic-style ceiling. Against the side wall, a kind of small wall has been raised
which almost reaches the ceiling, giving rise to a graceful corbel.

ROMANTIC TEMPERAMENT.
There are objects, fabrics, colors and shapes that unmistakably slip a romantic halo over the room. Pink or terracotta tones on walls or complements are a first step. Gauzes that descend from the ceiling to envelope the bed, creating a sensation of protection against the outside world, are another effective resource, as well as being economical. The enchantment of books, especially those which have survived a few generations of readers, and the delicacy or the softness of the colors and embroideries of bedspreads and cushions, are other ingredients conducive to romantic moods.

FURNITURE WITH A HISTORY.

Certain furniture or coverings have a heavy narrative charge, which will determine the rest of the decoration of the bedroom. For example, a filing cabinet or desk from an old office —when information technology was still a dream— will remind us of other times, when all work was carried out meticulously by hand. Meanwhile, an oriental-style bedside table, next to a classical bed with a canopy, will tell ancient stories of Orient and Occident, interweaving the two cultures. Also a wall where the bricks have been left visible will inevitably mark the style of the bedroom, leaving the indelible stamp of the rustic style.

CHROMATIC HARMONY.

Evidently, knowing how to combine and apply colors will determine the visual balance of the room. In general, in bedrooms the application of cool colors, blues and greens, is recommended for their relaxing properties. Although, like everything else, this is relative, given that the application of a certain color should not be considered in isolation, but should take into account the environment – like the orientation of the room and the quantity of light it receives-, the relationship with the furniture that decorates the room and the personality of its occupants, seeing that colors have the property of altering moods.

old flavors

Looking at these kitchens, the typical, and occasionally clichéd, expression, "warmth of the home" attains its full meaning. They are spaces that give off a homely flavor, recovering the old function of the kitchen as the center of family gatherings par excellence, where food is stored, prepared and cooked, the vicissitudes of the day are discussed, laughter is heard and problems are solved at the same time.

They are kitchens where a country atmosphere is recreated, in the purest rustic style, timeless standard of beauty. They seem to arise out of the past, like a reaction against the excessive introduction of technology and the impersonalization which currently reigns in avant-garde circles. Thus, there is a return to the taste for natural materials, mainly wood and fired clay, and for traditional manufacturing processes, where the hand of man intervenes directly, the mastery of the artisan.

By reproducing the characteristic aesthetics of old country houses, it is as if these centers of vital energy had lasted, immune to the evolution of the times, thus ensuring the survival of the most pleasant traditions, like the recipes that grandmothers pass on to their grandchildren, bearers of the family's culinary secrets. On the other hand, the introduction of electrical appliances or new generation elements (like aluminum or stainless steel), can be enriching as long as the combination is well-balanced, by generating a contrast that connects the past and the future. For the most purist spirits, who do not wish to renounce the comforts offered by technology, there is always the option of camouflaging the new electrical appliances with wooden panels.

Clay floors, closets with made-to-measure wooden doors, restored regal wooden tables, larders that maintain crockery and food in order, simple shelves that keep kitchen items in view, old tiles (or ones that imitate their designs), stone or ceramic sinks, notes of color introduced by the glassware or fabrics..., are all elements susceptible to awakening our old memories, and ever-remembered smells and flavors.

TILES OR PAINT.

As wall covering in the kitchen, both options are perfectly valid. Old tiles always transmit a more authentic flavor, which sends us directly to the past. Replacing the tiles with some kind of plastic paint is another economical solution which also offers good results. If we paint the kitchen in an ochre tone, it immediately acquires a more lively and luminous appearance. Whilst if we choose to whitewash it, the rustic spirit of old village kitchens will be preserved. Generally speaking, the most oft-used option is the combination of tiles, in the area of greatest friction, with paint in the rest.

FUSION OF ANCIENT AND MODERN.
Kitchens with a more contemporary style, which incorporate some up-to-date elements in their composition, also have the capacity to generate cozy atmospheres, especially when the room conserves intact the flavor of its old structure, like the essential wooden beams in the ceiling. Turning to a large wooden work table, to furniture with grille doors, to the invaluable presence of a larder, or to a modern teak furniture dining set, is always a good idea to maintain a certain warmth in the room, which counteracts the coldness of the more modern accessories.

BY THE WARMTH OF THE FIRE.

In the olden days, the kitchen was the center of life in the house, where the fire was the main source of energy, the element that generated heat, where food was cooked and around which the family gathered at the end of the day. The fascination that fire exercises is difficult to replace with any other system of heat or cooking, although the lack of time in the modern lifestyle has made the pleasant fireplace a distant memory, in favor of more practical systems. So that the mystical component of fire is not lost, if we are lucky enough to have a fireplace in the kitchen, we recommend keeping it, even if it is only lit on a handful of occasions.

INGENIOUS SOLUTIONS.

These two pictures show us two ways of equipping our kitchen with the necessary storage space, in a fast, simple, economical, practical and pleasant manner. What more can you ask for?
In the example on the left, all the kitchen utensils are visible. A piece of low built-in furniture, with the top covered with tiles, fulfills the double function of counter top and storage space. In the picture on the right, the same system of low closets has been used, but on this occasion, some coquettish curtains hide the items from view. Two creative solutions which, in addition, maintain the atmosphere of traditional sobriety. Ceramic and clay items complete the scene.

purify body and soul

Before, not so long ago, a bathroom was just that, a bathroom, whose location was usually relegated to the darkest and smallest place in the house. Now, the bathroom is much more than this, it has turned into a temple of health and well being, where we take care of the body and renew the spirit.

The space devoted to this room has multiplied, as has the imaginative effort devoted to its decoration and conditioning. Starting out from some specific cleanliness necessities which must be covered, it can even become a replica of the lounge, as if it were a room devoted to rest and the disconnection of the mind. Couches, rugs, sumptuous curtains, conservation of old wash basin models, recuperation of the ever-tempting bath with legs, hanging cut-glass lamps, marble, fragrances..., are small luxuries and pleasures that allow us to indulge ourselves, forgiving ourselves for these slips of vanity.

It is possible to recreate anything, from the impressive bathroom of a sultan's harem, to that which must have been used by the ancient kings of France, via those of rustic inspiration in large stately homes. The possibilities are infinite, as far as imagination can reach.

We all devote part of our time to daily personal hygiene. So why not turn those routine minutes into an act of renewal, taking advantage of the occasion to pamper and look after ourselves? A pleasant and comfortable environment will help us in the task of connecting our senses when we wake up and relaxing us at night in the antechamber of sleep.

The secret is to find the style that best connects with the sensibility of each person, with their way of looking at life, choosing those bathroom fittings and complements that best fit in with the necessities and intimate nature of each person. In this way, the bathroom becomes a private temple, where time moves slowly and mundane obligations do not exist.

PLAY OF GREENS.

The color green carries with it all the freshness of nature, with its comforting power. For this reason, the bathroom is the most ideal room to be coated with this color, especially when nearing the lighter tonalities in the range. A bathroom in green tones always reinforces its reinvigorating function, whatever its decorative style. In the picture above, the green tiles spread out from the ample built-in wash basin unit to the floor. The wall, on the other hand, has been coated with a coconut or sisal mat, generally used on floors, which contributes great warmth, although it is only recommended for bathrooms with excellent ventilation.

ODE TO THE BATHTUB.
What is it about bathtubs, with or without legs, that makes them the direct subject of multiple poems or romantic fantasies?
Perhaps it is their rounded shapes, the grace of the legs that support them, their evocative retro feel or their Hollywood connotations
of luxury and well being: long bubble baths savoring a glass of champagne. A fantastic adaptation to modern atmospheres
is to paint their exterior in vivid colors, coordinating with the rest of the decoration or giving rise to a strong contrast,
which brings out even more the beautiful prominence of its shapes.

IN THE ATTIC.

Sometimes, the reduced dimensions of the attic or the excessive slope of the roof rule out turning it into a bedroom
or a living room, but they are ideal places to install a bathroom. In this way, good use is made of this cozy space,
adapting the different bathroom fittings to the irregularity of the room. On the lowest side, where the roof ends, the bathtub
is usually situated, because taking a bath doesn't require much height. If the slope is so pronounced it does not permit
the fitting of a window in the wall, a good way of illuminating this area is to fit a skylight in the roof.

CLASSICS FROM A DIFFERENT PERSPECTIVE.
It is easy to turn around the elements belonging to the classical style, changing their old image for another that implies looking at them with more up-to-date eyes. Sometimes, we can change this classical perspective with a simple detail. For example, an angle presided over by a bathtub clad in white marble and some pink-colored curtains will no longer hold the same meaning if we finish off the framing with an Arab-style lamp. Painting the walls an intense pink color, putting down a fun rug, cladding the bathtub in earthenware tiles of different shades of pink, or covering the sink unit with natural stone of different shades, are other actions which supply a new vision of the bathroom.

FROM VERSAILLES TO THE SULTAN'S PALACE.
The space reserved for the bathroom gives plenty of opportunity to recreate mini-worlds within it, which reflect different philosophies of life, or simply the most varied tastes. From the baroque of the classical French style, with its chandelier and golden framed mirror included, to another which reminds us of "The Thousand and One Nights", with its individual use of arches, contrasting lights and colors, via others of great compositional sobriety or clear rustic influence or, on the contrary, more contemporary influence. There are as many possibilities as worlds we can imagine, the only requirement is that it be comfortable for its users.

A SMALL KINGDOM.

These pictures and the following ones show us how a bathroom can be turned into something very special, where it is possible to allow ourselves small luxuries and details inspired by our coquettishness or sybaritic tendencies, destined to increase the quality of our day-to-day life. The free-standing bathtub with legs, whose presence seems to fly beyond time, is a caprice we will never tire of looking at. An even clearer example of the bathroom as a temple erected for the care of our very selves, is to include a sofa or a couch with firm filling, where we can complete the regeneration produced by a pleasant bath, until we reach a profound state of relaxation and well being.

a perennial spring

Frankly, in a house surrounded by a beautiful garden or located opposite a plantation of vineyards, or in another which is in the middle of a cared-for Mediterranean-style forest, or which has panoramic views over a cliff where the waves crash, a large part of the work has already been done for us if we want to convert a terrace, a porch, a patio or a corner to have an afternoon nap or read outside, into a magical place. All you need is a love for nature and fresh air. The little details will do the rest.

Plants and trees play a fundamental role outside, as creators of a fresh atmosphere, full of life and warmth at the same time. There is nothing like enjoying a summer meal under a pergola covered with vine leaves or bougainvilleas, which project onto the table a refreshing play of light and shade, beneath which the diners are sheltered. It is also a fantastic experience to have an afternoon nap in a teak or wicker deck chair beneath a tree, or have an aperitif on a cozy porch.

The chosen exteriors reflect the adoption of different styles, each one with its particular way of communicating with the forces of nature. In some pictures, there is a predominance of a certain hippy aura or, to put it another way, what we imagine the patio or terrace of a typical country house in Ibiza must be like: with wild vegetation, a free environment, colorful, composed from recycled elements and with a light nostalgia floating above the atmosphere. Other exteriors are put forward as an extension of the lounge, with furniture and complements appropriate for inside. Also, the influence of the orient is felt is some suites for sitting down and chatting, transporting our imagination to dreamlike places In short, there are many ways of feeling the air, from the most rustic and in communion with the environment, to other more classical ways or those which attempt to tame the vegetation and characteristics of the terrain to their taste.

Be what may, the exteriors of our house are large windows open to the sky, whose mission is to make us feel eternally young, by creating the illusion of living in a springtime that never ends.

DIFFERENT WAYS OF SITTING IN THE OPEN AIR.

*The outside of the house is also susceptible to reflecting the most varied lifestyles, independently of whether it is in the city center
or in the countryside. Amongst many other styles, we can sit in the oriental style, on large cushions of different colors or on
chairs made from bamboo; another way, more traditional and awakening memories of the countryside, is to sit on wicker chairs,
as befits the dining room area; or we can also choose the classical style, either on suites of seats with cast iron structures,
specially made for outside, or on a comfortable sofa or armchair, which look as if they have been stolen from the lounge.*

BALANCE OF LIGHT AND SHADE.
To make the most of the terrace, and to be able to spend the maximum length of time in the open air, it is very important
to take into account the creation of different areas of sunshine and shade, which cover different necessities: direct sunlight
to tan ourselves in summer, or in the season in which the heat diminishes; refreshing shades to enjoy pleasant meals,
sheltered from the summer heat, or to read and sleep on summer afternoons, under the protection of the invaluable
canopy or awning. It is a good idea to fit curtains around the porch or deck, because they are a versatile and
aesthetic resource to increase or diminish the effect of the light.

MAKE GOOD USE OF THE RESOURCES.

*A cozy and comfortable atmosphere can be created in a very small space, as it is also possible that a terrain with a privileged location and size
can be completely lacking. The secret, shouted to the four winds, is to know how to get the most out of the available resources. That is,
if there is a leafy tree on the terrace, it will be obligatory to position the dining area under its branches. If, on the other hand, the outside area
is arid, we will protect it from the sun with a large sunshade or canopy, endowing it with visual freshness with plants and bamboo cane fences.
If our house, in another example, has stone walls, we can make good use of their coolness, situating a sitting or dining area next to them.*

THE COLORS OF EARTH.
Painting the walls of the porch with a color extracted directly from the earth, or with the right combinations, multiplies
the charm of this outdoor space. Thus, with only a few decorative elements we will achieve a very rich effect, like the pleasant
sensation obtained by a simple canvas deckchair or a cotton hammock, inseparable companion of after-dinner conversations rocked
by the breeze. Evidently, the most lively colors with the greatest powers of suggestion are those contributed by the plants themselves,
like a carpet of grass, which contributes a freshness both visual and effective to the atmosphere.

SWIMMING POOLS BY THE SEA.
Fresh water that gazes out onto the immensity of salt water. To boost the effect of the fusion between the water of the swimming pool and that of the sea, the best option is for the edge facing the sea to have an overflow system, creating the optical illusion that there are no limits between them both.

THE PURITY OF STONE.
Unpolished stone, in its pure state, deserves to be classified as truly beautiful. It takes us back to the beginning of time with its firm adhesion to the earth. Due to its imposing presence, simplicity should be the imperative for decorating the places where stone takes on a notable starring role.

CONTEMPLATIVE ATTITUDE.

These places invite an unhurried contemplation of nature, to observe how the leaves fall from the trees or to guess what figures the clouds represent. A light sofa with a cast iron structure whose curves form harmonious patterns, some simple iron chairs, the low wall of a terrace which becomes a rustic bench, a pleasant breakfast spot with impressive views. They are small gestures, isolated pieces, which have in themselves the capacity to create pastoral environments, where we feel in close contact with the outdoors and, consequently, with ourselves.

IN THE GARDEN OF EDEN.
The hand of man, with the help of the unstoppable life force of nature, is capable of recreating paradise, right here on Earth. Small versions of the Garden of Eden for private use, leafy orchards where we can hide ourselves from the rest of the universe. Vine leaves or bougainvilleas cling tightly to the pergolas or frameworks, creating a privileged viewpoint, an area ruled by the force of chiaroscuro, an ideal stage from which we would like to watch life go by, capturing direct visions of paradise.